FINDING GENIUNE INNER PEACE

through the power of forgiveness

by

Valerie Edwards

Published by Valerie Edwards

Copyright © Valerie Edwards 2016

ISBN: 978-0-9948738-0-4 Softcover
ISBN: 978-0-9948738-1-1 .EPUB format
ISBN: 978-0-9948738-2-8 .mobi format
ISBN: 978-0-9948738-3-5 .pdf format

Contents

Preface

Introduction

One Final Thought

Finding Genuine Inner Peace

Preface

There are many contributing factors that enable us to experience a state of genuine inner peace. Gaining freedom from negative emotions (generated from injustice, hurts, and traumas) through the power of forgiveness is an essential key strategy that *cannot* be bypassed. My hope is that the information contained within these pages will provide the understanding and tools to enable you to acquire the freedom you deserve to enjoy.

Finding Genuine Inner Peace

Introduction

Is it possible to consistently experience an inner peace that's *real*?

The answer is a resounding YES!

I invite you to come with me on a journey that will open doors to an inner freedom that you may never have experienced before. True pleasure and overwhelming joy is waiting for you. It may require courage, persistence, and honesty with yourself and others, but peace that pervades your entire being is worth your unrelenting pursuit.

For the purpose of this book, when I speak of experiencing inner peace, I'm referring to a peace within as you're going about your daily activities, no matter what is happening on the outside. Real inner peace is a state of being, not a momentary event that's dependent on outer circumstances. Those fleeting moments or hours of calm are wonderful. Enjoy and appreciate them when they come, but know there is a much more enduring, deep peace that's possible to experience.

One quality of real peace is that it's *alive* - not dead. I used to meditate using various eastern techniques in order to attain inner peace. I'd either fall asleep or I'd experience a "peace" that was dead by comparison with the peace I now experience. Feeling "nothing" is a poor substitute for the real thing. Real peace is accompanied by real joy, contentment, serenity and inner emotional stability, as well as freedom from anxiety, agitation, and other negative emotions. Peace is full of life at its best.

When I was meditating using eastern techniques, I didn't know I was just feeling nothing. It was certainly better than being anxious, in turmoil, confused, agitated, tense, inconsolable, depressed, numb, lethargic, angry, deflated, hopeless, paralyzed, and fearful. Not that I ever felt all those emotions at the same time, but feeling even one of them was awful.

I've written this book in order to share with you a necessary requirement for experiencing true inner peace. There was a time in my life when I was full of anxiety and other negative emotions and didn't know how to find the inner tranquility I was longing for. Let's just say it's been an interesting journey, but I've gained some powerful insights that I sincerely hope will help release you from whatever is preventing you from experiencing the peace you were designed to have. Ready?

Chapter 1

Symptoms of a Hurting Heart and Soul

You were designed to experience an ongoing wonderful inner tranquility. Our bodies, minds, and emotions were never created to accommodate turmoil for any length of time. We may manage to cope for a while, but eventually stress takes its toll. Medical doctors agree that stress, in all its varied forms, wreaks havoc on our bodies, minds, and emotions.

The first step in finding our way back to our originally designed state of being is to recognize and acknowledge the symptoms that indicate a lack of inner peace.

A symptom is like a flashing light on the dashboard of your car when it's running low on oil. The reason why car manufacturers design a warning system is to make drivers aware that their car is in need of attention. Ignoring these warning signals can have dire consequences.

Just as it would be foolish to ignore a flashing light on our car's dashboard, its foolish to ignore personal symptoms that indicate all is not well within. Wisdom is acknowledging that these symptoms are outward signs of an inward situation.

Even if you've lived with a negative inner situation for a long time, it's never too late to change. Don't let defeatist thoughts dissuade you from moving forward; thoughts like "I've tried to do something about this before and nothing's worked", or "I was born this way", or "I guess this is my lot in life". These statements simply are not true. Everything is possible if you believe it's possible. If you don't believe something is possible, you won't even try to find any answers or seek help from outside sources. If you can see that others have inner peace, then you know it's possible. If it's possible for someone else, then it's possible for you.

Following is a list of common symptoms of a hurting heart or soul. See if you recognize any that you are consistently experiencing.

- agitation
- anger
- anxiety
- bitterness
- confusion
- cynicism
- depression
- envy
- dread
- fear
- hate
- hopelessness
- impatience

- jealousy
- judgmental attitude
- lethargy
- maliciousness
- nervousness
- regret
- restlessness
- stress
- turmoil

This is by no means an exhaustive list but if you are experiencing any of the above, it doesn't take a rocket scientist to determine you're not experiencing complete inner peace. But for other reasons, a lack of inner peace is not always so obvious. Until you've experienced real inner peace, it may be difficult to know whether your "normal" is the real thing.

I remember one day when I began sensing a restlessness stirring inside me that was building energy with every passing minute. I decided to go for a walk instead of pacing in the house. I happened to be living in a semi-rural neighborhood at the time, which was a perfect environment to declare my thoughts out loud without the distraction of wondering if people might see or hear me. I felt I needed to give voice to whatever it was that was stirring inside.

For forty-five minutes I walked the neighborhood and declared to the universe that I was of value. I had a right to take up space and use up oxygen. I continued to declare anything related that came to mind. I wasn't aware of what I was accomplishing at the time but in actuality, what I was doing was declaring my absolute value as a human being and the right to be treated accordingly. I was part of the human race, uniquely created, and therefore of value - simply because I existed.

When I arrived back home, as I stood in the middle of my living room, I suddenly became conscious of feeling very, very different. So different, in fact, I thought to myself, "So this is what it's like to feel *normal!*" It was truly a transformational exercise I had undertaken and now I was feeling an inner peace that I couldn't have even imagined just a short time before. I hadn't realized how disconnected and unworthy I really felt in the recesses of my heart. The transformation was permanent and I am happy to say, I have grown in an even deeper, more encompassing inner peace since then.

Beginning in my early twenties, I had struggled with my sense of self-worth but didn't know how different my inner experience was from those who are healthy in this respect. A lack of self-worth is definitely a condition that robs us of inner peace. It can be a result of an accumulation of experiences or beliefs that have taken hold without us even being aware of how negatively we are being affected. We just know something isn't quite right. Although restoring a sense of self-worth is extremely important, it is a subject for another book and outside the scope of this one. My intention here is to help you become aware of your inner state and to find a greater measure of peace by focusing on the matter of letting go of past offenses. This will ultimately eliminate many of those troubling symptoms mentioned previously.

In the next chapter, we're going to delve into understanding one of the major symptoms in order to have a better understanding of what we are dealing with.

Chapter 2

ANGER

I used to have a recurring childhood nightmare of me trying to say something very important but when I opened my mouth to speak, nothing would come out. It was so frustrating and traumatic, I would start crying in my dream and then I would wake up.

I didn't understand, until much later in life, that this dream was a result of my upbringing combined with my own sensitive nature. The fact that I couldn't speak in my dream was a reflection of not being allowed to have a voice, of not being heard and therefore, not being affirmed to the degree I needed. An extension of this was that I didn't learn how to deal with anger in a healthy way. As a result, I grew into adulthood with plenty of unexpressed and unresolved anger. I was simply very out of touch with this emotion.

The Truth About Anger

Anger is a natural emotion. It isn't wrong to experience anger nor is it a bad emotion in and of itself. It's how you deal with it that determines whether it will have a negative or positive impact on your life and your relationships.

Because we often see the negative results of suppressed anger exploding on the television news or expressions of anger that are totally inappropriate, we may conclude that anger is a bad emotion to be avoided at all costs. *This couldn't be further from the truth.*

Built within every human being is a sense of justice, right and wrong, a sense of what is fair. Whenever our sense of justice is violated by others towards us or those we care about, anger is a natural response. Just imagine telling three five-year-olds that if they would come sit at the table, they each would get a cookie. If you gave two a whole cookie and one of the children a half cookie – believe me, you'll emphatically hear about how unfair this is from the one who gets the half cookie. And rightly so! The cheated child would have been lied to and treated unfairly.

Injustice can happen easily within families, schools, among peers, the workplace, government policies, social practices and so on. No one gets through life without experiencing this on some level. Living in a world with imperfect people, including ourselves, it's important to figure out how to deal with injustice in a way that keeps us free on the inside and doesn't suck us dry of our joy and peace.

Anger will <u>not</u> go away if ignored or suppressed.

Believing anger will go away if ignored is a mistaken belief. On the contrary, unresolved anger is stored in our souls, minds, and even our bodies. Besides the many negative emotional and mental states already mentioned, unresolved anger can produce an array of physical illnesses such as stomach ulcers, chronic fatigue, headaches, insomnia, and muscle tension - to name only a few.

Perhaps there have been times you were afraid to admit you were angry for fear of the consequences you might suffer if you made it known you were very unhappy with how things were done or said.

I used to believe if I expressed my anger or annoyance at someone, it would be the end of the relationship. Perhaps this had happened in the past, so I assumed it was just the way things were. This was totally unhealthy. There are going to be disputes in any relationship. If there are two people trying to relate and do things together, eventually something will be said, done, or disagreed upon that will require a resolution.

At one period in my life, I was "fortunate" to have a co-worker who annoyed me regularly. In fact, it was quite mutual. However, unlike me, he was able to easily express his annoyance, talk it out and move on. Eventually I learned, at least with this individual, that it was safe to express my own anger because I didn't need to fear that the entire relationship would be jeopardized. That truly was a healing relationship for me.

Note: You can't necessarily do this with everyone. If you can though, you know it's a healthy relationship on some level.

On the other hand, you may be so "programmed" to believe anger is bad, that you unconsciously prevent yourself from admitting you are angry. Your inner censorship acts more quickly than your conscious mind, resulting in a total lack of awareness of your true emotions.

Whether you acknowledge your anger at the time or not, it must be dealt with. If it isn't, it will eventually come out in other ways. Following is a more detailed list of symptoms related to unresolved anger.

Moodiness

Have you met people who "wake up on the wrong side of the bed"? Do you find yourself some days to be in a very negative frame of mind and you just don't seem to be able to shake it off? Sometimes it seems like there is a dark cloud over you, following you everywhere. This, my friend, is often a symptom of unresolved anger.

Depression

Much like moodiness, depression can be a symptom of many things such as emotional or physical trauma, but it can also be a symptom of unresolved anger. Severe depression can adversely affect your ability to function in general whether at home, work, school, or in relationships. It is a persistent sadness or loss of interest or pleasure in normally enjoyable activities. Besides the symptoms already mentioned, fatigue, insomnia, self-harm, avoidance of social interaction, loss of appetite and suicidal thoughts are some of the many symptoms of this painful condition.

If this describes you, please reach out for help. Find someone with whom you can confide in, who would be able to offer you help and guidance. There are help-lines, doctors, ministers, friends, and others who are willing and able to come alongside you during your time of need.

Disproportionate Anger

Have you ever been in a situation where someone reacted with an inappropriate intensity of anger to something that seemed to be a very small thing? You may be that person! Most of the time, people who react this way are unable to see themselves clearly. You can know there is a much deeper issue going on underneath the surface than the small matter that has set this person off.

Maliciousness

This is hate acted out. Cruelty to animals can escalate to cruelty to people. Malicious behavior is intentionally sabotaging others and inflicting physical, verbal, or any kind of abuse on others.

Bullying

Bullying is often the result of unresolved anger. If parents don't equip their children and teens to deal with their anger in a healthy way, they may end up directing their anger at "weaker" individuals, bringing much destruction to another's life as well as their own.

Sudden Anger for "No Reason"

Have you ever found yourself suddenly filled with anger when there didn't seem to be a reason? It just seems to come out of the blue. I would experience this regularly. But as a young adult, I decided I didn't want this to be part of my life. I recognized it wasn't healthy and I was determined to find out why this was happening to me.

I went looking for any book that could provide answers. (The internet didn't exist then – imagine that!) I finally found one that helped me understand that anger is *always* the result of something. It doesn't ignite from thin air. It is a response to some sense of injustice or offense to you or someone you care about. There is always a preceding reason you are experiencing anger.

Delayed anger is the result of an unconscious or semi-conscious need to avoid acknowledging to yourself or others that you are angry when the offense occurs. Your inner censorship shuts it down before you can consciously become aware you are angry. This reaction happens in milliseconds. However, since anger doesn't disappear on its own, it simply emerges later - sometimes days or weeks later - in which case you usually aren't able to connect it to the offense. The goal is to be able to acknowledge your angry feelings when the offense occurs.

As I began to be more aware of my emotions, the length of time between the offense and the time I felt anger became less and less until I was able to acknowledge and deal with my anger when the offense occurred. Wow! What a victory that was! No more sudden bouts of anger appearing out of nowhere. How empowering it was to be able to acknowledge that I was feeling angry the very moment it occurred and not be afraid of it. I could deal with the situation at the time in a mature, appropriate way and that was the end of it.

Bitter Sarcasm

Saying things to hurt people in a "joking" manner is nothing but disguised anger. It's a passive/aggressive approach to expressing one's anger. People may not be specifically angry with others they relate to like this...they just have an inner pool of anger that is spilling over into most of their relationships.

Regularly Reliving a Negative Situation

Do you find yourself often reliving an event in which you were humiliated by someone, or rejected, scorned, or wrongly accused? The possible circumstances are limitless, but you haven't been able to move on. You are continually rehearsing what happened, how you felt, what was said or what you should have said or done. This is clearly a symptom of unresolved anger or emotional trauma.

Escapism

There are all kinds of ways to try to avoid feeling the pain of negative emotions. Drug and alcohol abuse, eating disorders, oversleeping, watching endless movies or playing video games non-stop, workaholism, shopaholism, or any activity that's extreme in nature or time spent is often a sign of subconscious attempts to escape an emotionally painful inner reality. If you are engaging in an activity like this, be encouraged. There are things you can do and new ideas to believe in that will not only set you free from those destructive activities, but they'll address the source of those negative emotions once and for all.

Avoidance tactics are a dead-end road. They may bring temporary relief, but the consequences of engaging in long-term destructive behavior is just that – destructive to you as well as to those around you and to those who love you. If by chance you think no one loves you – you're mistaken. There is someone who loves you - you just don't know who that is yet. More about that later.

Chapter 3

Getting to the Root of the Matter

Every experienced gardener knows that in order to get rid of a weed, it must be entirely uprooted. Just removing the leaves won't kill a weed because as long as the root is there, life is being transported from the soil through the root and will continue to produce leaves. The same is true when dealing with symptoms of a hurting heart or soul. Simply trying to control or suppress symptoms does not bring permanent freedom. You may succeed for a while with will power or various coping mechanisms, but just like plucking leaves off a weed, the symptoms will eventually reappear.

In order to permanently free oneself from persistent negative emotions, one has to understand why those emotions are there in the first place. Although addressing the source of those symptoms may be scary and somewhat painful, the healing that occurs when properly dealt with is worth the emotional effort.

Injustice, Hurts and Trauma

An injustice or offense usually results in anger, which symptoms we have already dealt with in the previous chapter.

In this chapter we turn our attention to the other two thieves of inner peace, namely trauma and emotional hurts. Many times these happen in our childhood, but of course they can occur any time during our lifetime. Babies are not able to cognitively understand disturbing emotions of others in their environment, but they can pick these up on a deep level, which may have a lingering negative influence.

Another avenue for traumatic influence is the fact that very young children sometimes believe things that aren't true. For example, it's not uncommon for children of divorced parents to believe they are the reason for their parents' divorce or that the parent who leaves doesn't love them. This belief, although it may be entirely untrue, can become a deep-seated sense of guilt, shame, a sense of abandonment or any number of other crippling emotions. In adulthood, these individuals may not vividly remember or be aware of these events or circumstances, but symptoms later emerge indicating all is not well within.

As previously stated, symptoms are like flashing lights on a car's dashboard, drawing our attention to the fact that we need healing on the inside. If we uncover the underlying reason for their existence, we can gain freedom. I have been healed of many things from the past, but I'll share one dramatic healing to illustrate my point.

In my mid- twenties, I began to be aware that something just wasn't right within. I felt a general uneasiness and noticed that some of my reactions or interpretations of what people said or did just weren't healthy. For a number of years I tried off and on to figure it out, but I just couldn't put my finger on the issue.

Have you ever heard of the saying "It was a blessing in disguise"? A few years after my initial awareness of my inner uneasiness, I found myself in an ongoing situation that involved a particularly dysfunctional person - my blessing in disguise. This person was verbally hurtful and disrespectful to me, both privately and publically. I seemed incapable of sticking up for myself. Outwardly I just took it, but inwardly I was devastated. After many months of putting up with this behavior, I finally came to the end of my emotional rope.

I lived by myself at the time and one morning, after another disturbing encounter with this individual, I sat on my couch for two hours sobbing uncontrollably. "What was the matter with me? Why couldn't I stand up for myself? Why was I allowing this person to do this to me?" In between sobbing sessions, I vocalized my questions, my dismay, my sense of helplessness, and anguish. Then I said something that stopped me in my tracks. I pleaded, as if trying to convince the world, "But, I'm not @%$*&#!" It was a crude derogatory statement about me that I was disputing. The reason it stopped me in my tracks was the fact that I don't talk like that. In fact, I don't even think like that. Where in the world did that thought come from?

If I was now denying being @%$*&#, then I must have previously believed I was. As this revelation dawned on me, I recognized it was a degrading lie that had been embedded deep in my subconscious. I couldn't remember anyone ever saying that to me, but likely the concept had been communicated to me in other ways. How it came to be didn't matter at the time. The important thing was that somehow I had come to believe it, and it had lain deep in my soul, hidden from my conscious mind. The power of that lie had been alive at the core of my being, subtly influencing my every waking moment without my conscious awareness.

I immediately made a simple but passionate declaration that it was indeed a lie and I rejected it with all my being. By this time I was on my knees and I proceeded to flop down to the floor, utterly exhausted and emotionally spent. In the next few moments a brilliant insight was given to me. It came, I believe, from the Spirit of God.

It was revealed to me that this lie had grown from a "seed" into a "tree" in my inner life. The tree had been bearing all kinds of "bad fruit". The fruit was symptoms such as defensiveness, timidity, jealousy, a sense of inferiority, low self-esteem, a victim mentality, and so on. They were a compilation that made up my inner uneasiness.

The revelation continued. The moment I had recognized this belief was a lie and rejected it wholeheartedly, the axe had been taken to the root of the tree. In other words, the life and power of that lie had been removed and as a result, I was assured that the bad fruit would naturally disappear from my life without further effort.

This is exactly what happened. Just days later, the miracle of freedom from the tyranny of that lie began. I noticed that my reaction to a situation that came up was totally different from how I would have reacted before. Like a weed that had been entirely uprooted, the symptoms soon disappeared because they no longer had life support.

And my blessing in disguise? The next time this person made a sarcastic cutting comment towards me in front of a group of friends, I confronted them right then and there. They were so embarrassed, I was never mistreated by them again. This individual was a bully who had found a victim to torment. But the victim (me) had shed her victim mentality and was able to stand up for herself as any self-respecting person would.

That was it! I had regained my self-respect by releasing myself from a hateful internal belief that I hadn't previously known I had. I was able to freely forgive this person and I'm happy to say that years later, they also have found a great deal of inner healing and peace.

Beyond childhood events, trauma can be the result of any kind of emotional, physical, sexual, or verbal abuse. Accidents, war, crime, natural disasters, involvement with the occult, horror movies, loss through death of loved ones, and divorce, are only a few of the kinds of events that can leave a lingering inner brokenness.

As well as those symptoms listed under anger, trauma can also result in the following:

- compulsive behavior
- disease
- facial tics
- inability to trust
- insomnia
- mental illness
- nightmares
- panic attacks
- post-traumatic stress disorder
- social maladjustment

Again, this is by no means an exhaustive list, but if you recognize and acknowledge that you are exhibiting any of the symptoms mentioned so far, be encouraged. ***Awareness is the first step to freedom.***

In the next chapter, we'll discuss how hanging onto these negative past experiences prevents us from enjoying the wonder of true inner peace.

Chapter 4

How the Past Can Hold You Captive

I recall one day observing an acquaintance who seemed to be in all respects an intelligent, mature individual suddenly acting like a nine-year-old having a childish snit. I wondered how this was even possible, but I had witnessed it with my own eyes!

When an issue is unresolved, we can become "stuck" in our emotional life. Whenever a new situation occurs that "reminds" us (often on an unconscious level) of that original event, a button gets pushed. The new event acts like a trigger, setting off the same type of reaction that occurred during the original event. The current emotional response may not seem rational and likely isn't. That's because the unresolved issue is keeping us from becoming a fully mature individual.

Unfortunately, if this is you, you may be the last one to see it. Be kind to yourself and listen if those closest to you are telling you that your behavior is childish. It probably is, because there is a pocket in your soul where you are stuck in your past. Don't beat yourself up over it. Simply decide to deal with it and move on. We'll talk about how to do that in the next chapter.

Retaining a grudge or holding onto bitterness, resentment, hate, and anger has serious negative consequences. It's like drinking poison, hoping the other person will die. The other person may be completely unaware of what they've done or how you feel about it, but these powerful emotions affect you very negatively.

Ask yourself, "What do these emotions accomplish?"

Answer:_____

_____

_____

_____

_____

I hope you recognize that negative emotions accomplish absolutely nothing positive for you. The other person isn't being punished by your emotions, but you certainly are. By holding onto them, you perpetuate your own torment which negatively affects you emotionally, mentally, physically, relationally and possibly even financially.

When we get a sliver in our little finger, it's only our little finger that hurts. But if left there, it affects our whole body. And as long as it remains, it can affect our emotions, our ability to concentrate, extend patience to others...everything. How much more will pervading negative emotions affect one's life?! They are much more powerful than a sliver in your little finger.

In some cases, if you hold onto these emotions long enough, they can become part of your identity. You may even hesitate to part with them because you might wonder who you would be without them. Be assured that once you are free from them, you'll never miss them.

Strongholds

When you keep rehearsing an event, with the same thoughts producing the same feelings, you are creating a stronghold. What is a stronghold? It is a strong holding pattern in your mind and emotions.

A stronghold can be a good thing or a bad thing. An example of a good stronghold is a firm decision to be honest in your dealings with others. A stronghold like this will make you resistant to temptations to lie, resulting in others trusting you to be a person of your word. You'll also never have to fear being discovered in a lie. Do you see how a good stronghold, like being honest, can bring peace into your life? If you don't lie, you'll have peace with others and peace within.

A bad stronghold has the opposite affect. Every time you rehearse a negative event, bringing to life the negative thoughts and emotions or making vows that are based in fear or hate, the negative pattern is strengthened. Examples of vows made out of hate or fear are, "I'll make that person pay for doing that to me" or "I'll never trust another person again". Continual rehearsal of this kind will keep you in a negative emotional and mental holding pattern that prevents your soul from moving on, and prevents you from experiencing the inner peace that could be yours. Holding on to past hurts keeps you from growing into a fully mature, free individual.

In the next chapter, I discuss how to break the grip of negative strongholds.

Chapter 5

Letting Go

Letting go is synonymous with forgiveness. Forgiveness is a term not commonly used in our current world, but it's a vital concept we need to understand so nothing will stand in our way of obtaining inner peace and freedom.

What forgiveness is <u>not</u>.

Forgiveness is not saying that what was done or said is okay. It is not okay for others to treat you disrespectfully, lie to you, cheat on you, steal from you, bully you, or anything that treats you in a way that is less than honoring, loving, and respectful. You are a person of worth, no matter who you are. You have value just because you are a human being. Yes, you! I can hear some of your inner voices saying something quite different. But the truth is, you are of value, period.

Low self-esteem is almost universal to various degrees and although you may feel this way, there is also another part of you that is screaming to be valued. That's because whether you feel like it or not, you were created with inherent value. It isn't earned. You have value simply because you exist.

I'm going to take a short rabbit-trail here and talk about a little piece of wisdom that's dear to my heart.

You may have heard of something called "the golden rule". It originated with Jesus, who said it was the second greatest commandment. It's simple yet profound. **Do to others as you would have them do to you.** In other words, treat others in the same manner you would want them to treat you. If the whole world followed this one guiding principle, we'd almost be living in heaven. But alas, we are not.

I remember driving home at dusk one evening when I noticed something unusual on the road. I quickly pulled over to check it out. Sure enough, it was a fat wallet. When I got home I checked the ID, found the owner's phone number and gave her a call. She had been riding on the back of a motorcycle and hadn't noticed her wallet had fallen out of her knapsack. Besides several pieces of ID, there was a lot of cash that she would have been devastated to have lost. She was one happy and grateful young lady and I felt great for having made her day.

Much of the time, it's quite obvious what the right thing to do would be. But whenever I find myself in a grey zone, meaning a situation that isn't cut and dried, I ask myself this question: "How would I like to be treated if I were on the other end of this?"

Sometimes, situations happen so fast that we act out of our default beliefs which aren't always perfectly aligned with the golden rule. I've made many mistakes myself. But if you have the opportunity to take some time to ask yourself this question before you act or speak, you'll spare the other person and yourself a lot of pain and in many cases bring real joy to others and yourself.

Ok, I've said my piece...back to the main issue.

Forgiveness is not downplaying an offense when you are actually hurting on the inside. This one is similar to the previous definition of what forgiveness is not. The difference is that your reasoning is trying to take over your feelings. When it comes to offenses, it's important to acknowledge your feelings. If you are not okay inside, don't intellectually try to convince yourself otherwise. This is when you need to really listen to your emotions. It may not make sense to others or even to yourself, but you need to honestly acknowledge your true emotions.

You can't deal with emotions effectively if you are in denial. They need to be acknowledged because emotions don't disappear. Emotions are energy. If negative emotions aren't released in a healthy, appropriate manner, they simmer underneath and will surface again. You can count on that.

Forgiveness does not mean that you trust that person again or continue to put yourself in a bad situation. For instance, suppose every time you get together with a certain individual, they verbally tear you apart and put you down. Just because you may have forgiven them to set yourself free from the pain of their torment doesn't mean you should continue to expose yourself to them. Unless you are able to confront them and they change their behavior towards you, it probably is best to forgive them and avoid them if at all possible.

What forgiveness is.

Forgiveness is letting go of your right to punish the other person. You are in essence making a decision - "I will not hold this offense against you." It's trusting that their actions will ultimately be dealt with but you yourself are letting them go. It's the opposite of taking revenge. If a higher authority such as the police, a principal, your boss, your parents, the justice system, or God deals with the other person, they are in a position to do that. But you are relinquishing your right to inflict punishment on them yourself.

Oh, did I say it was easy? Simple...yes. Easy...not usually. Necessary for you to obtain inner peace? Absolutely! Let's look at how to do that in the next chapter.

Chapter 6

Forgiveness Starts with a Decision.

Making a decision to let go and move on is one of the most powerful decisions you will ever make in your life. It will change your life for the better in ways you probably can't imagine right now, but you will never regret it. In fact, you will look back and be able to say it was a defining moment in your life.

Victim or Victor

Ask yourself this question, "Do I want to be a victim or a victor in life?" No one wants to be a victim but that is what we choose by default if we don't take control and make a decision to let go of those negative emotions. Letting go is firmly in our control. We may have been victimized by someone else, but we can choose not to have a victim mentality.

How can you tell if you have a victim mentality? The "victim" is constantly blaming others or making excuses for their own poor choices or behavior. "My life is like this because so and so did this to me, my parents did that to me, my boss treated me this way"... and so on.

The unfortunate reality is that blaming others gives our power away. If we blame others for our state in life, then we believe they have control. If <u>they</u> have control, then <u>we</u> do not. This results in feelings of helplessness and hopelessness. When we feel helpless and hopeless, we don't believe we can do anything to change our lives. But this simply is not true.

Victim-thinking is deceptive thinking. "Victims" wear emotional and psychological glasses that taint how they see the world interacting with them. They interpret circumstances, the universe, and most other people's actions under the assumption that everyone and everything is basically against them. People are out to mess with them, treat them badly, steal from them, put them down, and deny them their rights. Other people can never win with "victims" because "victims" are always interpreting other people's motives with a negative slant.

A perfect illustration of this mindset was played out by a tenant in the downstairs suite of a house a couple had just purchased. They had a two-week window to replace the old carpets upstairs, do some painting, and move the washer and dryer to a different location in the house before they moved in. A few days after the move-in, the tenant came to their door to express her anger for all the noise that had been made which had prevented her from getting proper sleep. The new owners had no idea she was on a night shift, trying to sleep by day, during those two weeks. Although it would have been near impossible to have arranged things differently (carpet layers and other trades people don't generally work at night) it was a very unfortunate situation.

When they realized what had happened, the new homeowners sincerely felt bad for her and apologized, assuring her that it was a one-time situation and would not be a continual occurrence. But there was no consoling her. They could tell by her response that she was certain they were just mean-spirited and wanted to make her life miserable. She refused to speak to them for the next two years! Because of her victim mentality, she created her own emotional prison by assuming the worst and held on to her poisoned view of them by keeping a grudge for the remainder of her stay in their suite.

Unfortunate things happen. And, yes, sometimes people do intentionally wrong us. Others may have played a very negative role in our formation as a person or hurt us in a bad relationship, a work situation, or any number of circumstances could have happened to us beyond anyone's control. ***However, it's not what is done to you or happens to you that determines who you are or will become. It's how you respond to your experiences of life that makes the difference.***

Are happy, successful individuals people who have never had bad things happen to them? No one, no matter their position in life, has grown up without disappointments, injustices, perhaps betrayals, and losses. The possibilities are endless. But people at peace with the world live in a state of inner peace because they have chosen not to cling to their negative life's events. They have made a decision to forgive, let go, and move on.

Two children can grow up in the same horrible environment. One ends up on skid row, the other becomes a success in life. Circumstances beyond your control and people's poor choices will affect you, but it's what you do with these situations that determine how you come through them and whom you become.

Think about all the famous people who had more money, talent, and good looks than they knew what to do with. Some have died an early death because of a drug overdose or suicide. Others have become philanthropists, using their money and fame to help others. **It's not the money, its not the fame, its not the outward appearance; its what's inside a person that makes the difference. It's your inner life; your thoughts, attitudes and beliefs of your heart and mind that determine whether you live a life of inner peace, happiness, and fulfillment or a life of inner turmoil, torment, and despair.**

It all comes down to choices. When you make a choice, you make a conscious decision to act or react one way or the other. Decisions are acts of the will. They don't require emotion – decisions require resolve. Resolve often comes as a result of an emotional experience, but resolve, itself, does not require emotion. It requires a clear-headed act of your will.

Most people prefer to stay in their comfort zones. Reacting how you've always reacted is easy but doesn't move you forward if your reactions are proving to be a negative factor in your life. It's often only when situations become unbearable that we are driven to make choices to better our situation. The ability to choose is one of the defining abilities of humanity. You have a free will. I encourage you to use it for your good! Use your resolve - your will - to make a decision that you are going to take responsibility for how your life turns out. You may not know how to make your life better yet, but once you make that decision, the "how" will come.

If you are ready to take responsibility for your life and choose to pursue inner peace, on the next page is a declaration you can make that expresses this desire.

Forgiveness Starts with a Decision

I, (state your full name), make a solemn decision today to take responsibility for my life. This means taking responsibility for how I react and respond to what has taken place in my past as well as whatever comes my way in the future. I choose to seek inner peace with all my heart and because I make this decision, I make a positive declaration that it will be mine.

Chapter 7

A Matter of the Heart

Although forgiveness starts with a decision - a matter of your mind and will - it doesn't end there. You must take it from your mind and bring it to your heart to truly forgive. Forgiving is not just saying the right words. That's just lip service. They're empty words if they aren't heartfelt.

Forgiveness comes from the heart and is expressed through words. Therefore, forgiveness must reach to the depths of your heart where these emotions reside, in order for your forgiveness to release them.

It's somewhat of a mystery as to how it happens, but genuine forgiveness unlocks the place in your heart or subconscious where these emotions reside. As you forgive from your heart, using words of forgiveness, the negative emotions are released and replaced with peace or the opposite of what you were feeling.

Many years ago I found myself repeatedly replaying a scenario in my mind that had taken place years before. While I was at university, a housemate had said some very hurtful and untrue things about me to the other housemates. Years later, there I was, still hurt, still wounded from the knowledge she had done this. By this time I was living in a different city and who knows where she was living, but I decided I didn't want these hateful emotions taking over anymore.

By this time in my life I knew that if I could forgive her from my heart I would be set free. It wasn't necessary for me to physically see her. It was only necessary that I forgive her. So one day when I was alone, I solemnly said out loud, "I forgive you, Megan" (not her real name). There! I had done it!

The following day, I suddenly found myself mulling over the same old scenario with the same old hate. I was perplexed and disappointed. I had sincerely forgiven! What was the problem? So I got quiet and in the most honest, sincere sense of the words, I said out loud again, "I forgive you, Megan." "For sure, that should take care of this", I thought, as I continued with my day. The next day, to my utter dismay, I found myself steaming over the same scenario with the same hate! But I was determined. I thought, "OK, I'm going to forgive her again but this time I'm going to imagine her walking into the room and as I look into her eyes I know I will have completely forgiven her if I feel only peace and love in my heart towards her." So again, I dug as deep as I could, and said with every earnest fiber within me, "I forgive you, Megan." Then I imagined her coming into my room, and as I imagined looking into her eyes, there was only peace and a real love for her in my heart. I was free at last! I went to bed that night full of joy because of my newfound inner liberty and peace.

I learned something very important from that experience. If you want to be completely free, *it's necessary to forgive to the depth of your hurt.* What I mean by this is that forgiveness must go as deep in our soul as the hurt has gone. For instance, suppose you are shopping and someone slightly bumps your arm. They apologize. You respond with, "No problem". This is hardly an offense but you get the picture. It's easy to forgive someone when the hurt is almost nothing. But when the hurt is deeper, your forgiveness must go to the depth of your emotional pain in order to set yourself free.

This is what happened with me concerning Megan. She had deeply hurt me. Although I had sincerely forgiven her the first time, it hadn't reached to the depth of my hurt. But each successive time I forgave, I was able to go deeper, even though I really couldn't feel I was going deeper. I just knew it was the right thing to do. My perseverance paid off and by the third time, I was able to completely forgive. I was rewarded with peace and freedom. The hateful emotions are gone and except for recounting this story, I have never given that situation another thought. Now that's freedom!

Some hurts are so painful and deep that it may require great persistence on your part to reach complete freedom. In the next chapter I give you some helpful techniques for letting go.

Chapter 8

How to Forgive and Helpful Techniques for Letting Go

Once the decision is made, the act of forgiveness is actually quite simple. Below is a sample statement of forgiveness you can either say to a person or just say out loud when you are by yourself. Just thinking this statement does not have the same effect as speaking it out. The spoken word is very powerful.

"(Name of the person), I forgive you for (describe the wrongs done to you). I give up my 'right' to judge you. I let go of my desire to make you pay or hurt for what you did."

In whatever way you gauge your progress in forgiveness, seek completion. If all it takes to accomplish this is one session – wonderful! But if you find that you are still carrying the negative emotions concerning an issue, then you know you still have some work to do. Don't be disappointed, discouraged, or tempted to give up. Persist in forgiveness sessions until you know you are free. Inner peace is priceless and worth every effort you make to obtain it.

Helpful techniques for letting go

As is true for any new skill, the more you do it, the easier it becomes. In the meantime, until you've made it a way of life, you may find that a simple forgiveness statement may not achieve the desired results for those more difficult situations. It can be helpful to accompany your statement with creative actions. The following are some suggested forgiveness exercises.

Symbolic Burning or Shredding
Take a piece of paper and make a list of all the offenses a person has done to you or the effects that a particular circumstance has had upon you. Or if it's one situation, write detailed paragraphs of how they hurt you. Get it all out on paper. Then get a match or lighter, go to the fireplace or lean over the sink. In a little personal ceremony say, "I forgive you (name) for all of these things." Light the piece of paper. It's a symbolic representation of the fact that you are forgiving this person, letting the offenses go, not to be brought up again. (If it's not possible to burn your piece of paper, tearing it up into little pieces will accomplish the same thing.)

The Imaginary Chalkboard
This technique is easy to do anytime, anywhere because you don't have to physically do anything. Picture the offender sitting in a chair facing a chalkboard. You are standing at the chalkboard with chalk and brush in hand. You write on the chalkboard all the offenses this person has done to you. You then declare that you forgive them. You then see yourself taking the brush and wiping away the offenses, leaving a clean chalkboard.

In addition, depending on the relationship, you may want to imagine going to that person and embracing them in a hug.

The Conversation

Grab two chairs and place them facing each other. Sit in one chair and imagine the person you want to forgive sitting in the chair across from you. Talk to them as if they were there. Tell them how you were hurt or angered. Get it all out and then forgive them.

Writing a Letter

Take a pen and paper or get on the computer and write a letter to this person telling them how you feel. Leave it for a day at least and maybe more. Once you've gotten all of your feelings out and had a forgiveness session by yourself, you may decide not to send the letter or you might decide to modify it significantly.

The danger with settling disputes or confronting someone via letter, texting, or email is that only the words are conveyed. Since it is generally accepted that approximately 55% of verbal communication is composed of body language, 38% is intonation and only 7% is the actual words, an email, text, or letter will be omitting important communication elements.

On the other hand, a letter can be an effective way of communicating if talking it out isn't possible. Writing a letter can give you time to cool down and gives you the opportunity to choose your words carefully. This is especially true if you are the kind of person who finds it difficult to communicate well while under stress or when emotionally wrought. Use wisdom.

Empathy
Often times it's easier to forgive when you understand that the other person involved has issues of their own. Try to put yourself in their shoes or see things from their perspective. For instance, perhaps a parent over-controlled you as a child. Perhaps something happened which had a great negative effect on them, resulting in their misguided need to try to control everyone around them so they could feel safe, fulfilled or whatever was their sense of lack. As an adult, you come to understand why they are so controlling. This understanding can result in compassion for them instead of anger.

Understanding them doesn't change the fact of how badly they may have treated you. But trying to understand why a person does what they do or why they are the way they are can make it much easier to forgive.

Gaining a Different Perspective
Just like flying in an airplane over a city gives you a different perspective of the same city you see by walking the streets, a different perspective of a hurtful situation can entirely change the way you respond.

At one time in my life I had been influenced by a segment of the feminist movement I'll call "the angry ones". I'm all for gender equality, so in that respect you can call me a feminist if you want. But there is a segment of that movement made up of women who are angry and bitter towards men in general. Fortunately, through some helpful biblical teaching I received in my early adulthood, I had a profound revelation that men and women had truly been created equal in value. This realization dramatically changed my attitude towards men.

Equality became my reality, not a theory that I had to convince men to believe. The fact that I am an equal, neither less than nor better than but different in certain respects, became my deep abiding identity. Immediately my anger turned into a mild sadness for the poverty of mind and heart of men who didn't see me the way I now saw myself. If men treated me less than I deserved, that was their problem, not mine. (This same revelation is true for racial and ethnic differences. We may be different but we are all of equal value as human beings.) What wonderful freedom and peace this new understanding brought to my life and my relationships with men.

Personify the Emotion
After forgiving the other person(s), another technique is to personify the negative emotions and send them away. In other words, address the emotions as if they were an entity you can speak to. Use your own words but here's an example of what you can say:

"(Name your emotion), I release you from my being. I no longer want you to have a place in my mind, emotions, heart, or body. There is no longer any room for you. I direct you to go from me now." Visualize this emotion leaving every fiber of your body, soul, and mind, evaporating into thin air. Sometimes breathing deeply and exhaling deeply is helpful as you visualize this emotion leaving you.

"I now invite peace to come and live in my heart, mind, emotions, and body. Peace, you are welcome within me. I embrace you. I love you. You are my friend, safe place, my keeper." Again visualize peace coming into your body, mind, and soul as you deeply inhale.

Note: If all the negative emotions don't leave or come back, don't be discouraged. Keep on doing this as the occasion arises. The negative emotions will eventually lose their grip on you the more you convince yourself that you no longer want them. Not only do you not need to be a victim of others or circumstances, **you don't need to be a victim of your own negative emotions.** I'm not suggesting denial. Denial is saying you don't have a particular emotion when you really do. Sending an emotion away is an exercise of personal decision, not fantasy.

These forgiveness techniques are only suggestions that may be helpful. If you find something that is more effective for you, then by all means use it.

Chapter 9

Signs of Freedom

When true forgiveness takes place, different people experience different things. Sometimes you might immediately feel a peace and an ability to breathe deeply, sighing with relief. Other times there is a sense of a heavy weight being lifted off your shoulders or heart. You may feel emotionally lighter. Tormenting thoughts or voices will cease. Sometimes there isn't much of an immediate feeling, but later you discover that you are happier or you aren't burdened by thoughts of that person or event any longer.

Emotional Transformation Related to Memories
The most satisfying result of fully forgiving is when you remember the incident or situation but your anger or painful feelings do not accompany the memories. Forgetting what you forgive is a fallacy. Forgiving doesn't magically wipe out our memories, but it does change the emotions connected with those memories. If you feel peace within when you remember negative events of the past, then you know you have totally forgiven.

If you still have sorrow, anger, or pain when you remember the event or person involved, then there is still a need to forgive to a greater depth. Even though these emotions may have diminished, don't sell yourself short by settling for less than total freedom and peace regarding any individual instance. Every time the memory comes up and you notice these emotions, take time to get alone with yourself and have a forgiveness session.

Another indication you have completely forgiven is when you notice you have no need or desire to bring the offense up with the offender or with your friends who know about it. In fact, it doesn't even cross your mind any more. It's not that the event is completely forgotten, but the memory no longer surfaces because it doesn't have an emotional hold on you anymore. If you still find yourself every once in a while jabbing the other person by bringing up the old topic again, then realize that you have not completely forgiven from your heart.

Inner Peace and Well-being
This is the greatest benefit of being set free from negative emotions tied to past events. As you deal with each of the negatives of your past, which may take a while, there comes a pervading tranquility to your inner being that is simply pure joy.

Chapter 10

Staying Free for the Rest of Your Life

Now that you know how to set yourself free from the past, you will want to keep yourself free in the future. This chapter provides wisdom for dealing with offenses that are bound to come your way. As long as you are alive, your ability to quickly forgive will come in handy whenever you need it.

Humility is a key character trait to develop.
In the matter of forgiving others for their offenses, it always helps me to remember that I am not perfect either. Unless you are like no one else on the planet, it's wise to acknowledge that you, too, have done some insensitive, dumb things that hurt others in the past and probably will do so in the future. That doesn't make you a horrible person. That simply confirms that you are a human being - part of the human condition that's flawed but loveable, uniquely valuable but sometimes blind or self-centered. If we can give ourselves some slack for an occasional act of insensitivity or even stupidity, then we should extend the same grace to others.

It's important to consider whether you have contributed to the situation in question. If you have, then humbly acknowledge that to the offending party *before* confronting them about their behavior. This will set the stage for a positive outcome. Most people, when confronted with an attitude of humility, will be quick to apologize. Often they aren't even aware of how deeply they may have hurt us.

Do you need to discuss the issue(s) with the offender? In my experience, the best strategy for working out issues is to forgive the person in your heart *before* you talk with them. When you no longer carry the load of emotional anger or hurt, you can approach the other person with more control of your emotions, which in turn enables you to choose your words more carefully.

After privately forgiving the other person without their presence, you may feel that a discussion is unnecessary. But if it's something that is likely to occur again or was quite grievous, then set up a meeting to intentionally discuss how you were affected by the other person's actions or words.

Consider if the person is able to meet with you or do they live in another city or country. Consider how long ago it was and if you can even contact that person. Are they even aware that they hurt you?

If I believe I need to have a difficult conversation with someone, I'll often rehearse what I'll say until I feel it's the best way that will allow the other person to understand and receive my message. Unloading your emotions privately prior to your conversation will help prevent further damage from taking place by avoiding unkind words.

It's extremely important to use phrases such as, "When you said or did (that), it made me feel like (this)." Don't say or imply, "You are a horrible person because you did such and such". That is attacking their identity. It's their *behavior* that you are taking issue with.

Keep the issue only between you and the offender.
One of the worst things you can do is talk to everyone else about your feelings except to the individual in question. All this does is poison other peoples' minds. Perhaps what was said or done is a total misunderstanding and once you speak to this person, everything is okay between the two of you. But now, all the other people are still thinking poorly of the other person. Don't do this. Remember the golden rule. If you did something bad but apologized for it later, would you want your whole sphere of friends to know about it? Or would you rather the offended person work it out with you confidentially and give you the opportunity to make it right?

There are exceptions to this of course, like when the offense is criminal in nature. Then it's appropriate to go to the police, or if you're young to tell your parents or those in authority.

Forgiving strangers is important too.
Sometimes strangers offend - people you'll likely never meet again and have no way to contact. The person who dangerously cuts you off in traffic comes to mind. If this is the case, then just forgive them on your own. I can't stress this enough: ***Forgiving is more for you than the other person.*** The other person may never even know they've done anything wrong. Forgiveness sets you free within from hate, grudges, revenge, and a host of other tormenting emotions. It may seem contradictory, but forgiving others is an act of loving yourself.

What if the other person doesn't agree they've done anything wrong?

Let's face it, the most satisfying outcome we can dream of is when the other person admits they have wronged you and says they're sorry or asks your forgiveness. It takes a lot of maturity and humility to admit you're wrong. When you know their apology is sincere, it's easy to forgive and move on. But what if they sincerely don't agree they have wronged you? Or what if their issues cause them to be nothing but defensive; blaming you, making excuses, making threats or walking away from the conversation altogether? Sometimes you've already had discussions with an individual who refuses to take responsibility for their actions, or refuses to acknowledge that you could be offended by their actions or words.

When you've done everything you can to work it out but you've come up against a brick wall, it's time to accept that there is nothing more you can do. If they never take ownership of their part in the situation, then that is their loss, not yours. The truth is, you don't have to remain in an attitude of bitterness and grief just because they don't ask for forgiveness. That's the beauty of forgiveness. You can cut yourself free by making a choice to forgive, let go, and move on whether the offender admits to their part or not.

What to do when the people who have hurt you are deceased.

You don't have to forgive someone in person. Forgiveness is more for you than it is for the other person. So go ahead and forgive using the techniques given in Chapter 7.

What to do when you are the offender.

When you know you've hurt someone in any way, it weighs heavily on your heart and mind. It's a burden your soul was never meant to carry and indeed, you don't have to. It takes great courage, but the thing to do is go to that person in private and say you're sorry. Ask forgiveness too, but be forewarned; since most people don't know what forgiveness is, few will be able to offer it. However, most people will accept an apology – take that as their forgiveness. This can restore your relationships and garner a greater respect for who you are.

There was a time when a past relationship started weighing heavily on my heart. I had worked at a youth hostel under a supervisor a few years prior to this and had at times spoken to him with disrespect. I felt I needed to go to him and ask for his forgiveness. I popped by his workplace one day and asked to speak with him privately in his office. When I asked his forgiveness for being disrespectful, he was a bit speechless. He didn't seem to understand what had become so clear to me about the power of forgiveness. He didn't think forgiveness was his to give.

Although I knew he could have offered it, I accepted his response. At least I had done what I could do. I was able to walk out of his office with a clear conscience, which was worth its weight in gold.

If families lived in an attitude of forgiveness, there would be far fewer divorces, teenage alienation, and generally more peace and harmony in the home. Parents make mistakes in their parenting, children disobey their parents, wives and husbands say things that hurt. We need to quickly ask for forgiveness when we know we are in the wrong. It is a life-changing moment when a parent asks their child for forgiveness. This communicates genuine love, humility, and honor of the child. They will respect you all the more and know that you respect them. When couples are able to quickly ask and give forgiveness, they don't allow bitterness to take root. Offenses, if not taken care of, will multiply until the weight of them causes walls of protection and separation to build that can have devastating effects on a relationship. There is a scripture in the bible that says: "Don't let the sun go down on your wrath". In other words, endeavor to resolve an issue before the day is over, especially with whom you live.

Sometimes it's not possible to ask forgiveness in person. Writing a letter can be a great way to communicate with someone. You have time to compose your thoughts and rewrite it to say it the best way possible. I did this with my parents after I had left home. There is so much children take for granted. When we enter adulthood and acquire a more mature perspective, we will no doubt recognize that our misdeeds were too numerous to count. Getting a letter like that from a child including an expression of appreciation for all they've done can be very healing to a parent.

What if the person you ask forgiveness of doesn't offer it?

It isn't what you would hope for but sometimes people haven't the understanding that you are gaining in this book to know how powerfully freeing forgiveness is. If you've genuinely asked for forgiveness and the person doesn't respond positively, then you can be satisfied that you have done what you can do and leave with a clear conscience.

On the other hand, it may be that something more is required. Appropriate actions should accompany genuine apologies. Perhaps restitution is in order. For example, if you lost an item you borrowed from a friend, you could buy something similar to replace it. Restitution isn't always possible or appropriate but if it is, it shows you really care. Do for them what you would like to have done for you. Perhaps you did something to cause someone to lose their trust in you. Forgiveness doesn't have to take long, but restoring trust usually takes some time. You may have to prove your trustworthiness in various circumstances before the other person is willing and able to trust you again.

What if you have resentment or jealousy towards someone but you recognize they haven't wronged you?
This one's easy. Don't say a word about it to them. This is your issue and really has nothing to do with them.

Many years ago I remember being quite envious of a certain young woman who seemed to have everything going for her. She came from a fairly well-to-do family, was beautiful, had a lovely personality, and was a talented musician. I, on the other hand, did not have the benefit of her background. I certainly didn't have her beauty and I recognized that I had a lot of issues that needed working out. Yes, I was quite envious and it brought considerable discomfort to my soul.

I realized I needed to have a genuine attitude change but wasn't sure how that was going to happen. Often when we are envious of someone, we just want to tear them down or talk negatively about them to others. Wrong, wrong, wrong!

One day as I was pondering my angst over this situation, I felt guided to pray for her well-being and for her to experience success in every way. I also felt I was to sincerely compliment or encourage her as the occasion would arise. Oh, that was tough! She already was so blessed in life and I was supposed to bless her even more? However, as I followed through, almost overnight, the envy disappeared! In the process, I discovered that although she looked like she had everything together, she still had insecurities like everyone else.

This is what I learned: never compare yourself with others. It leads only to despair or pride. There is always someone who is more talented, richer, better looking, stronger, smarter, more popular or whatever! On the other end of the spectrum, there's always someone less fortunate than you in every way. But each human being is of unique value. Each has their own story, their own value to bring to the world. Cherish your uniqueness. It's not what has been done to you or what has been handed to you in life that determines who you are. The important thing is how you handle what you've been dealt.

Can I forgive myself?
You most certainly can. You may have done many things that are weighing heavily on your heart. You may also have neglected to do things that you feel you should have. Regret is a terrible thing to live with, but the wonderful truth is that you don't have to.

Besides asking the other person's forgiveness (if it's possible or appropriate), the most effective way to deal with the burden of regret is to forgive yourself. Sometimes regret doesn't even involve hurting others, but rather disappointing yourself. Perhaps you made a foolish decision that cost a small fortune, a relationship, or a dream. Or maybe you didn't take action towards a golden opportunity that has since passed you by.

Most people find it much easier to forgive others than themselves but that is really a form of either pride or self-loathing. Don't let either keep you from the freedom you deserve and really want. You are in as much need of forgiveness as anyone else. The process is the same as forgiving others. Get alone - look in a mirror if you like, and say to yourself, *"I forgive you, (say your name), for (describe the situation)."*

Chapter 11

The Power to Forgive

Would you consider yourself open-minded? Would you say you are respectful when listening to others' perspectives? I hope you've answered "yes" to the above questions because I'm about to introduce you to something you may never have seriously considered before. Since you've gotten this far, I'm hoping you'll open your mind and heart to hear something that holds for you the possibility and opportunity for the greatest freedom yet. I've kept the best for the last.

Sometimes the pain, the hate, or other feelings that are keeping you trapped seem too difficult to relinquish. What do you do then? This is where grace comes in.

Grace is another concept like forgiveness that is seldom appreciated in our present culture. One of the definitions of grace is 'the enabling power of God'. The bible says that "God gives grace to the humble". And elsewhere it says, "Ask and it will be given to you". If you are having difficulty forgiving, then you can ask for help from a higher power. I don't mean just any higher power. I mean the power of the Creator of the universe!

There actually is a Prince of Peace. He is most famously known as Jesus Christ. Here is a quote of what He said about inner peace. "I give you my own peace and my gift is nothing like the peace of this world. Don't let your hearts be troubled and don't be afraid." (John14:27) Jesus wants you to be able to experience the kind of inner peace that brings joy and isn't dependent upon outer circumstances. In another place in the bible, He said that He came to give "life to the fullest" and that includes wonderful inner peace.

In order to receive this gift of freedom and to experience abiding inner peace, He said that we must forgive others of their offenses toward us so that we could be free from the torment of bitterness, hate, and envy. In what is known as 'the Lord's prayer', Jesus taught us to forgive those who have sinned against us (done things or said things they shouldn't have)... and in another place He said, "Forgive others so that your Heavenly Father will forgive you." Here's the thing: Jesus promises to forgive you of your sins when you ask Him to (1 John 1:9) and if that's the case, He asks us to do the same for others.

The fact is, God loves you – no matter who you are, no matter what you've done or what has gone on in your past. The greatest act of forgiveness was communicated two thousand years ago when Jesus died on a cross to take the punishment we deserved for the things we've done that have hurt others. He did this so we could be forgiven and spend eternity with Him as well as experience His love, joy, and peace while living here on earth. The thrilling thing is that He not only died but He rose from the dead to live forever. Whoever chooses to believe in His act of love and forgiveness towards them will be given the gift of living eternally with Him. (John 3:16)

Right now He is knocking on the door of your heart and inviting you to open your heart to have a relationship with Him so you can be completely forgiven and live with Him forever. If you would like to receive Jesus into your life, say the following prayer sincerely from your heart.

Heavenly Father, I come to You admitting that I haven't always lived as I should. I ask You to forgive me of all my sins (wrong doing, speaking, and thinking) and cleanse me from within. Your Son Jesus Christ died on the cross and rose from the dead so that my sins would be forgiven and that I could be reconciled with You, my Creator. I ask You, Jesus, to be my Savior and the Lord of my life. I choose to follow You and ask You to fill me with the power of the Holy Spirit. I now declare that I am a child of God. I am saved in Jesus' name. Amen.

If you sincerely prayed that prayer, angels are rejoicing in heaven and you are now a follower of Christ! You have started on the most amazing journey of your life and will never be the same. I prayed a similar prayer more than 30 years ago. All the principals I've shared in this book are based on God's wisdom. Jesus has set me free from too many things to mention. I wouldn't trade what I now have and experience for all the riches of the world.

A few helpful tips
As a follower of Christ, find a bible in a newer translation (like the New International Version) and start reading the gospels Mathew, Mark, Luke, and especially the Gospel of John. Find a church or other believers and share with them that you have decided to follow Jesus. Pray to God who hears your prayers. Prayer is just talking to God and listening for impressions in your heart from Him. Ask for the power to forgive everyone that has hurt you.

If you don't want to forgive someone, be honest. At one time there was a person that I just didn't have it in me to forgive. However, I did want to please God and I knew it was His will for me to forgive. So I backed my prayer up to where I could be sincere. I prayed, "Lord, I know You want me to forgive (name withheld) and You know I really don't want to. *But I am willing to be made willing to forgive.*" Without me having to do anything, God answered that prayer by changing my heart in a matter of days and I received the power to forgive.

It doesn't matter how badly you are stuck. If you're honest with God and want His best by doing His will, He will get you unstuck so you can move into sincere forgiveness and experience the resulting freedom and inner peace that you were created to enjoy.

One Final Thought

Can we forgive God?
That's a very interesting question. First of all, God is good. He always has been and always will be. He is love. He is perfect, just, faithful and He never changes. There is nothing He has ever done or will do that is wrong. But in our limited human perspective and understanding, God gets blamed for a lot of things He is not responsible for. Even natural disasters, which are labeled "Acts of God" by insurance companies, are labeled as such because of erroneous human assumptions.

Jesus is the exact representation of the character of God. How He dealt with a storm at sea gives us an indication of God's perspective on weather catastrophes. In the gospel account of an incident at sea, Jesus is asleep in a boat with His disciples when a storm erupts. The storm is so violent that the disciples begin to fear for their lives. These are seasoned fishermen who had a great deal of experience with adverse weather conditions. If they feared for their lives, we can be confident they were in desperate peril of drowning. Upon being awakened by the disciples, Jesus immediately commanded the wind and water to be still. This was not the action of someone who caused the storm but rather someone who cared about the lives of those in danger. Jesus said, "The thief (referring to satan) comes only to steal, kill, and destroy; I have come that they may have life, and have it to the full." (John 10:10).

The truth is, God created the world as a paradise for people to enjoy. He also created us with a free will so that we wouldn't be robots but would have the freedom to choose to have a genuine relationship with Him and live a life of love. Unfortunately, people choose of their own free will to do, say, and think things contrary to the perfect love of God. This is what is known as sin, which ultimately is the source of all suffering in the world.

So to answer the question, "Can we forgive God?"...yes, if it helps to set ourselves free from resentment and anger towards Him. But if we seek to know who He really is, eventually we'll come to understand that He was never the source of our pain and neither is He in need of forgiveness.

He is the Rock, His works are perfect,
and all His ways are just.
A faithful God who does no wrong,
upright and just is He.

-    *De. 32:4*

www.ingramcontent.com/pod-product-compliance
Lightning Source LLC
Chambersburg PA
CBHW071642050426
42443CB00026B/909